Tuning In

This is a non-chronological report and could be read in any order. The notes that follow take you through the book in order from beginning to end, but you could also ask the children to select a particular section from the contents page and report back on that, or ask them to research particular aspects of the book using the index.

Start by asking the children to skim through the book and tell you what they think it is about. How do they know? Can they use the contents page, headings, illustrations and index to find evidence?

Front cover

Let's read the title – do you know what 'mythical creatures' are? (*creatures from stories and myths*)

Can you think of any mythical creatures?

Where would you turn to, if you wanted to check quickly if these creatures are mentioned in the book? (*the index or possibly the contents page*)

Back cover

Let's read the blurb together.

Have you heard of any of these mythical creatures?

Do you think this sounds like an interesting book?

Why, or why not?

LESSON 1 (PAGES 2–13)

READ

Read pages 2 to 5

Purpose: To read the contents page and the opening section.

EXPLORE

Pause at page 7

Looking at the contents page, what different sections are there in the book?

Which do you think looks most interesting, and why?

Which page would you turn to if you wanted to find out about mythical creatures from different countries around the world?

(A) Use these questions to gain evidence for AF4.

Why do you think people liked to make sculptures and tell stories about mythical creatures?

Can you find the special name for an ugly stone creature on a building? *(gargoyle)*

Tricky words (pages 4 and 5)
If the children struggle with 'sculptures' (page 5), 'gargoyle' (page 5) or 'bestiaries', model how to break the words down into syllables to help with reading them. Talk about what the words mean and look in the glossary (page 24) to find the word 'sculptures'. (AF1)

Contents

3

What Creature is That?

Many creatures in stories are mythical. This means that they are not real, and never have been. These strange creatures often have special powers.

For hundreds of years, people have told stories about mythical creatures. Long ago, people made **sculptures** of mythical creatures and put them on buildings.

An ugly stone creature on a building is called a gargoyle.

This sculpture of a winged lion guards the city of Venice in Italy.

Hundreds of years ago, people in England and France made special picture books about mythical creatures. These books were called bestiaries.

Today, mythical creatures appear in stories, films and games.

4

5

READ

Read pages 6 to 9

Purpose: To find out some differences and similarities between giants and trolls.

EXPLORE

Pause at page 9

Can you tell me some differences between giants and trolls?

How might they be similar?

If you had to find the page about trolls quickly, what would you use to help you find it?

 Use this question to gain evidence for AF4.

Check that the children can read the words with less common graphemes, e.g. 'people', 'beanstalk', 'frightened' and 'friendly'.

 Use this pointer to gain evidence for AF1.

Giants and Trolls

Giants

Giants look like people, but they are much bigger and stronger.

Hagrid, in the *Harry Potter* stories, is a half-giant.

In stories, the hero often defeats the giant by being clever. In the fairytale *Jack and the Beanstalk*, the giant is cruel and stupid.

In *Jack and the Beanstalk*, Jack climbs the beanstalk to the giant's castle. The giant tries to kill Jack, but Jack cleverly escapes.

A one-eyed giant is called a Cyclops.

People blamed giants for things that frightened them. They said that giants caused thunder by shouting and stamping. Some people also said that giants made mountains and valleys by stamping on the ground.

6

7

Trolls

Trolls can be big or small.

Large trolls usually live alone in mountain caves. They have bad tempers and keep to themselves. The grumpy troll in *The Three Billy Goats Gruff* lived alone under a bridge.

Trolls often have big ears and noses.

Small trolls also have bad tempers, but they often live in groups.

Tove Jansson with models of the Moomins.

But not all trolls are grumpy. Tove Jansson wrote about a family of trolls called the Moomins. The Moomins are happy and friendly creatures, and they love adventures.

8

9

5

READ

Read pages 10 to 13

Purpose: To read the section about mythical beasts and report back to the group on the one you think is most interesting.

EXPLORE

Pause at page 13

Which mythical beast did you like best?

Why?

Which do you think is the most beautiful?

Which would be most dangerous?

Check that the children can read the words with less common graphemes, e.g. 'treasure', 'ancient' and 'character'. Model how to read these if necessary.

 Use this pointer to gain evidence for AF1.

Please turn to page 14 for Revisit and Respond activities.

Tricky word (page 12)
The word 'phoenix' may be beyond the children's word recognition skills. Tell them this word if necessary.

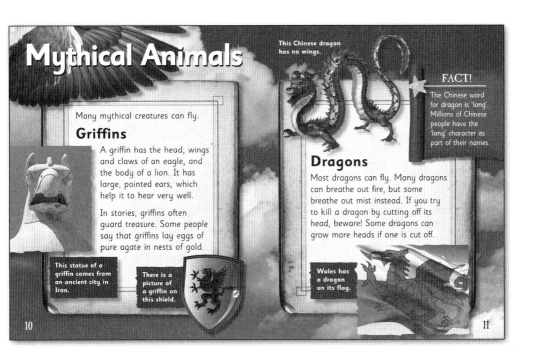

Mythical Animals

Many mythical creatures can fly.

Griffins

A griffin has the head, wings and claws of an eagle, and the body of a lion. It has large, pointed ears, which help it to hear very well.

In stories, griffins often guard treasure. Some people say that griffins lay eggs of pure agate in nests of gold.

This statue of a griffin comes from an ancient city in Iran.

There is a picture of a griffin on this shield.

This Chinese dragon has no wings.

FACT!
The Chinese word for dragon is 'long'. Millions of Chinese people have the 'long' character as part of their names.

Dragons

Most dragons can fly. Many dragons can breathe out fire, but some breathe out mist instead. If you try to kill a dragon by cutting off its head, beware! Some dragons can grow more heads if one is cut off.

Wales has a dragon on its flag.

10

11

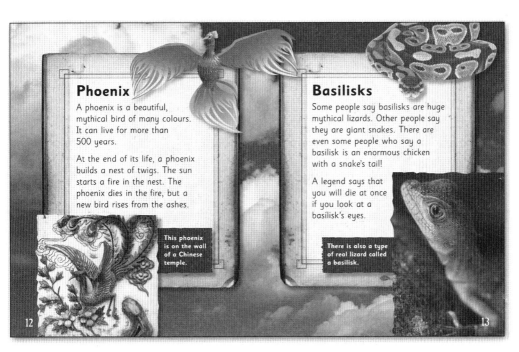

Phoenix

A phoenix is a beautiful, mythical bird of many colours. It can live for more than 500 years.

At the end of its life, a phoenix builds a nest of twigs. The sun starts a fire in the nest. The phoenix dies in the fire, but a new bird rises from the ashes.

This phoenix is on the wall of a Chinese temple.

Basilisks

Some people say basilisks are huge mythical lizards. Other people say they are giant snakes. There are even some people who say a basilisk is an enormous chicken with a snake's tail!

A legend says that you will die at once if you look at a basilisk's eyes.

There is also a type of real lizard called a basilisk.

12

13

7

LESSON 2

Recap lesson 1

What kinds of information can we find in this book?

How would you find the information about dragons as quickly as possible?

 Use this question to gain evidence for AF4.

READ

Read pages 14 to 17

Purpose: To find out about unicorns and mythical 'little people'.

EXPLORE

Pause at page 17

What magical powers did people think unicorns had?

Why do you think the author included the chart on page 15?

Do you think this is a good way of giving us a lot of information without taking up much space?

 Use these questions to gain evidence for AF4.

How many different sorts of 'little people' does the book tell us about?

What bad thing did some people think pixies might do?

8

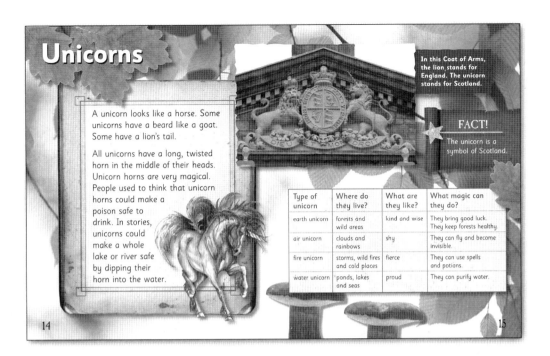

Unicorns

A unicorn looks like a horse. Some unicorns have a beard like a goat. Some have a lion's tail.

All unicorns have a long, twisted horn in the middle of their heads. Unicorn horns are very magical. People used to think that unicorn horns could make a poison safe to drink. In stories, unicorns could make a whole lake or river safe by dipping their horn into the water.

In this Coat of Arms, the lion stands for England. The unicorn stands for Scotland.

FACT!
The unicorn is a symbol of Scotland.

Type of unicorn	Where do they live?	What are they like?	What magic can they do?
earth unicorn	forests and wild areas	kind and wise	They bring good luck. They keep forests healthy.
air unicorn	clouds and rainbows	shy	They can fly and become invisible.
fire unicorn	storms, wild fires and cold places	fierce	They can use spells and potions.
water unicorn	ponds, lakes and seas	proud	They can purify water.

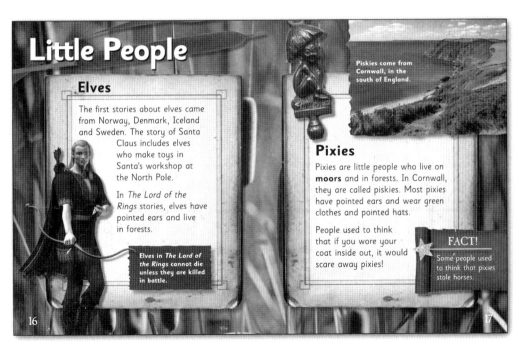

Little People

Elves

The first stories about elves came from Norway, Denmark, Iceland and Sweden. The story of Santa Claus includes elves who make toys in Santa's workshop at the North Pole.

In *The Lord of the Rings* stories, elves have pointed ears and live in forests.

Elves in *The Lord of the Rings* cannot die unless they are killed in battle.

Piskies come from Cornwall, in the south of England.

Pixies

Pixies are little people who live on **moors** and in forests. In Cornwall, they are called piskies. Most pixies have pointed ears and wear green clothes and pointed hats.

People used to think that if you wore your coat inside out, it would scare away pixies!

FACT!
Some people used to think that pixies stole horses.

READ

Read pages 18 to 23

Purpose: To read the information about mythical creatures from different countries, and choose one to tell the group about.

Tricky words (pages 18 to 21)
There are several tricky words on these pages, including 'kraken' (page 18), 'bunyip' (page 19), 'guards' (page 20) and 'sasquatch' (page 21). Many of these are decodable, but they are unfamiliar so the children may need help to split them into syllables in order to read them. Model how to do this if necessary.

Mythical Creatures of the World

Every country has its own mythical creatures.

Kraken

The kraken is a sea monster from Norway. It is like a giant octopus that attacks ships.

Real giant squid may have caused the legend of the kraken. Giant squid can grow longer than 10 metres, and they are sometimes caught by fishing boats.

This kraken is trying to sink a ship.

18

Bunyip

A bunyip is a water monster from Australian **Aboriginal** stories.

Bunyips live in swamps, rivers and **billabongs**. No one knows what they look like. They may have a tail like a horse and flippers like a walrus.

19

Tengu

A tengu is half human and half bird. It hatches out of an egg, and lives in the mountains and forests of Japan.

Tengus have wings and a long nose. They can speak without moving their lips.

This statue of a tengu guards a temple in Japan.

20

Bigfoot

Some people in America and Canada say that they have seen a creature called Bigfoot.

It is up to three metres tall and covered in hair.

In 1967, two men filmed what they thought was a Bigfoot. People still argue about whether the film shows a real Bigfoot or a man in an ape suit.

Beware — Bigfoot about!

FACT

The Native American name for Bigfoot is sasquatch.

21

Pause at page 23

Which type of creature did you choose?

Can you sum up why your creature is interesting, in one or two sentences?

Do you think that any of these creatures might be real?

On pages 22 and 23, can you find two words where the letters 'ie' are pronounced 'ee'? (*'believed', page 22, and 'pieces', page 23*)

 Use this question to gain evidence for AF1.

READ

Read page 24

Purpose: To think about the purpose of the glossary and index.

EXPLORE

Pause at the end

Is the glossary a useful thing to have in this book?

Would you have known the meanings of these words without it?

What sorts of words are in the index? (*names of mythical creatures*)

Why do you think the author put these words in the index?

 Use these questions to gain evidence for AF4.

Loch Ness Monster

Some people believe a monster lives in Loch Ness, a very deep lake in Scotland.

There are lots of stories of people seeing a large creature in or near the lake. The creature is sometimes called Nessie.

People who don't believe in Nessie say it is an otter, a seal, a dolphin, an eel, or even a swimming elephant!

Some people say they have taken photos of Nessie.

Loch Ness is in the Highlands of Scotland.

There are many statues of Ku in Hawaii.

Ku

Ku is a Hawaiian god who visited people as a man or dog.

He ate many people, so some men killed Ku with spears and clubs. They cut him into two pieces which were turned into stone.

22

23

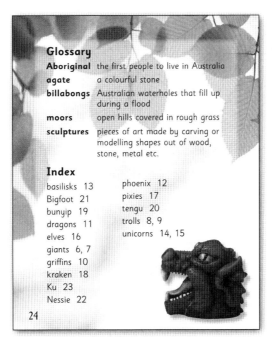

Glossary

Aboriginal the first people to live in Australia

agate a colourful stone

billabongs Australian waterholes that fill up during a flood

moors open hills covered in rough grass

sculptures pieces of art made by carving or modelling shapes out of wood, stone, metal etc.

Index

24

After Reading
Revisit and Respond
Lesson 1

- Have a race between two groups of children, to see who can find the information about griffins first. Ask one group to use the index and the other group to flip through the book using headings and illustrations. Which way is quickest? What are the good points about each way? Which way would be best if you were trying to find a small piece of information in a long book, or in a book with no pictures? (AF4)

- Ask the children to collect all the names of mythical creatures from the first half of the book (to page 13). Encourage them to group the names in different ways – e.g. by alphabetical order, by whether the name is easy to read or not, by whether they have heard of the creature before. What other ways of grouping the names can the children think of? (AF1, AF4)

- Check that the children are reading fluently and independently by asking them to choose a page of the book and read it aloud to a partner. Check for appropriate pace and expression, and model fluent reading for them if necessary. (AF1)

Lesson 2

- Encourage the children to find different items in the book by using the index – you could have a race to see who can be first to read out what the book says about bunyips, basilisks or Ku, for example. (AF4, AF1)

- Ask the children to list the non-fiction features that the author has included in this book (e.g. contents, index, glossary, section headings, photos, a table, captions). Can they think of any non-fiction features that are not included? Could the author have made the book better by including some other features? (AF4)

- Check that the children are reading with understanding by playing a 'twenty questions' game based on the book. The children should take turns to 'be' one of the mythical creatures in the book; the others should then ask questions to find out which mythical creature it is. Encourage the children to stick to questions that can be answered with 'yes' or 'no', and to use information from the book. (AF1, AF4)

Follow-up

Independent Group Activity Work

This book is accompanied by two photocopy masters, one with a reading focus and one with a writing focus, which support the main teaching objectives of the book. The photocopy masters can be found in the *Fantastic Forest Planning and Assessment Guide*.

PCM Gold NF 2.1 (*reading*)
PCM Purple NF 2.2 (*writing*)

You may also like to invite the children to read the story again, during their independent reading (either at school or at home).

Writing

Guided writing Write a character profile for one of the mythical creatures in the book, including information about what the creature looks like, any magical powers, where it comes from, etc. Add a labelled diagram showing the different parts of the creature.

Extended writing Use books and the internet to research another mythical creature, e.g. from Greek mythology. Write a new section for the book based on this creature.

Assessment Points

The questions in this Teaching Version will help you to assess children's attainment within a range of Assessment Focuses (AFs), but particularly AF1 and AF4. See the *Fantastic Forest Planning and Assessment Guide* for more information about the AFs.

Word Recognition and Language Comprehension

- Check that the children can read the text fluently by asking them to read parts of it aloud, paying attention to the punctuation and using appropriate expression. (AF1)
- Check that they can read words with less common graphemes, such as 'frightened', 'people' and 'believed'. (AF1)
- Check that they can identify some of the book's non-fiction features and use contents, index and headings to find their way around the book. (AF4)